Also by Ben Behunin

Remembering Isaac, 2009
Discovering Isaac, 2009
Becoming Isaac, 2010
Forget-me-notes, 2011
Borrowing Fire, 2012
Put a Cherry On Top, 2013

Ben's books are available through www.benbehunin.com, Amazon.com and wherever above average books are sold.

THE LOST ART OF WOOING RABBITS AND OTHER WILD HARES

A Collection of Poems and Photography by Ben Behunin

To Alana —

The Lost Art of Wooing Rabbits
and Other Wild Hares

A Collection of Poems and Photography by Ben Behunin

Copyright © 2014 By Ben Behunin

All Rights Reserved

Published in the United States by

Abendmahl Press
P.O. Box 581083
Salt Lake City, Utah 84158-1083

ISBN 978-0-9838025-7-0

Photographs by Ben Behunin
Design by Bert Compton

THANKS TO—

Rachel & Troy, Martin & Becca, Elyse & Rick, Dave & Marisa; who shared with me their love for poetry and inspired me to try my hand at it.

To Lynnette for believing in me, and to our children, Isaac and Eve, who put up with me and still pretend I am funny.

IDEAS ARE LIKE RABBITS,
YOU GET A COUPLE
AND LEARN HOW TO HANDLE THEM,
AND PRETTY SOON YOU HAVE A DOZEN.

—JOHN STEINBECK

PRELUDE

From the time I was a child, poetry has largely been an enigma to me. Even as I aged, I found it generally difficult to approach, much less, understand. Of course there were exceptions: Shel Silverstein, Dr. Seuss, and even songwriters like Paul Simon. But for the most part, poetry was intimidating and unapproachable—stuff, it seemed, that required an English degree, perhaps even a PhD, to appreciate.

But last year something changed. Sometime last fall, I heard two-time poet laureate, Billy Collins, interviewed on NPR. Billy read several poems from his recently released anthology. His poems were fresh and approachable—not at all the tangled messes of words and obtuse ideas I had experienced with poetry up until then. His poems were almost more like short stories, but they made me smile. I think it was that day, if not the next, that I sat down and wrote my very first poem. I discovered it was fun and gave me a chance to write without committing to the hours usually necessary to get myself into "the zone" required for novel writing.

Shortly after I wrote my first poem, a friend randomly called to ask if I liked poetry. She explained that several mutual friends were forming a group to share and discuss poems and their poets. She invited me and my wife, Lynnette, to join.

Lynnette and I quickly learned that we were vastly the least poetically experienced in the group. Some of our friends, we learned, grew up memorizing poetry. Others had been writing poems since high school. All of them knew what they liked and came ready to share what they had discovered. Some of the poets I had heard of. Many more, I had not. But I realized very quickly that I had been too swift to judge poets and their products, and thus starved myself of the simple joys that can be found in this creative, often personal art form.

I began buying poetry books, mostly used books from second hand bookstores. I began asking friends, writers, and English majors what I should be reading. All of them made suggestions. Some were exciting. Others left me wondering. But overall, the experience has been enlightening and uplifting.

Not being an English major, I don't know the rules of poetry, which is good, because if I had, I probably would have been even more intimidated. But poetry, I've discovered, is art, and art tends to break rules, flowing uphill some days and rushing through stop signs. I like that.

As readers of my novels have asked me what I am working on next, it has been fun to watch their faces register surprise when I tell them about my poems. Based on my own experiences, I am not expecting everyone to love them, but I hope this collection will offer you a chance to take another look at poetry. If nothing else, I hope it will inspire you to slow down for a minute in your fast-paced lives and look at life a little bit differently.

Cheers,

[signature]

December 2014

CONTENTS

Wooing Rabbits	16
...There is a Season	17
The Truth About Imported Crocodiles	18
Finding Words	19
Vitamin D	20
Ten Minute Segments	21
Worthy of Honey	23
Words That Rhyme	24
Juab County	26
Selective Interpretation	28
The Optimist	29
Ode to Silence	31
Wisdom	32
Low Fat	33
Other Fruit	34
The Truth In the Shadow	35
Flying Lessons	36
Alchemy in Motion	37
Vacation	38
Watching Melons	39
The Alarm	40
The Revolution of Living	41
Rent-a-family	42
Masters of Strategic Communication	44

A Decade Early	46
Pumpkin Pancakes	47
Forgotten Picnics	48
A Toast To a Sunday Afternoon of Boredom	49
A Seed of Hope	50
Wishes	51
Acceptable Ignorance	52
Absence in Presence	53
The Slow Way	54
Again to Ping and Pong	55
No Remorse	56
The Value of Laughter	57
Light	59
Afflictions of a Part-time Writer	60
Jesus Doesn't Wear Wingtips	61
Trade in Value	62
Stretch	63
Studio Visit	64
Ode to Ginger Ale	65
Silencio	66
Shoulder Patrol	67
4 Things	68
Cicada Interlude	69
Linger Longer	70
Monsoon @ 5 am	73
Conversation At The End Of The Day	74
Listening	75
Late Night Lamentations	77
A Summer Poem	78
The Truth About Cheese	79
Practice	80

Blowing Smoke 81

Jealous Lover 82

Trading Life 83

Easy Living? 84

Skidding Sideways 85

Pacific Coast Dreams 87

Van Winkle's Hair 89

Practical Solution #419 90

Hopes and Promises 91

Searching for Balance 92

A Too-Bright Moon 93

Prepaid Funerals 94

Muffled by Laundry 95

The Easiest Answer 96

Ode to Small Reminders 97

My Place 99

Peaches 100

Opportunities 101

Waiting On The Inevitable 102

I Never Considered 103

Fifty-nine Cents 104

Plans 106

An Atypical Alphabetical Alliteration 107

Memories @ 1 am 108

A Jar of Clarity 110

Mid-life Medicine 111

All the Magic That Surrounds Us 112

Mapping a Day's Journey 114

Below Average 115

Yoga Pants 116

Dandelions in the Sun 117

Autumn's Seduction 118
Living With Itch 119
Early Birthday 120
Advice to English Majors.. 121
Ovation.. 123
Things to Remember 124
Somewhere In Between 125

WOOING RABBITS

This is a poem
that might not have been written
except for the fact that
I neglected at least three
seeds of decent poems yesterday;

swept away under the proverbial rug
in my **frantic chase** of lesser things.
And by the time I came back 'round to them,
the over-scheduled day had CHASED them
back into their holes,

frightened rabbits who might never come to visit
my garden again;
not that I want to *encourage* the
running amuck and devastation of my garden,
to be overrun by herds of hungry rabbits,

nibbling at the lettuce and the
tops of the carrots so that **extraction**
can only be accomplished with the aid
of a SHOVEL instead of being easily
pulled up with the NAKED HAND.

But perhaps it would be good to
plant some arugula along the
fence line of my garden to
tempt those clever rabbits
to come to breakfast, and LINGER

through the day, feeding *untormented*
on the SACRIFICIAL VEGETABLES I have planted for them,
hoping to **atone** for the years of neglect,
when I have chased them away
with the SHOTGUN OF LESSER THINGS.

...THERE IS A SEASON

I am tired of the gray smog
that fills the valley with gloom
clogging off the beams that provide
the sunlight, so I shall not write about it.

Instead, I will write of springtime
and flowers, and leaves—budding from
the skeletal trees who will soon
remember they are still alive and will
desperately try to hide their nakedness.

And when I am done with that,
I will write about summer fun,
and the song of crickets
and the night sky with its river
of stars that flows from horizon to horizon.

And perhaps later, when I have grown
tired of summer, the sweltering heat,
the easy living, I will write about
how the chilly nights have
painted the foliage all the warm colors of summer

to help us remember
the good days as the snow returns,
once again to the mountains, and
smog fills in the valley, leaving me to dream
of better, brighter days.

THE TRUTH ABOUT IMPORTED CROCODILES

I remember hearing that the Chinese
like to import crocodiles and use them
as aphrodisiacs—a word I had to
look up when I was younger because
I wasn't sure what it meant,

and even when I did, I could
not understand how a soggy, toothed
swamp thing could
produce a feeling of longing
when eaten with fried rice.

I have seen crocodiles,
or at least their primordial
cousin, the alligator,
when I lived as a boy in Florida,
where no open water
was safe from the infestation.

I remember wondering, as I
would stare across the pond
in my backyard, if the gators
migrated on the legs of mosquitos
and other water-born insects,
finding homes in ponds far away

and if this were the case
why the Chinese would need
to import crocodiles and other
amphibians to make them
feel sexy when all they
needed was to import more mosquitos from the swamps
where the monsters lived.

But I remember my answer came
one day as I stood at the
edge of the pond; dressed only
in my cut-offs, looking for
snakes and realizing there is
nothing sexy about feeling like a
feast for the pesky skeeters.

FINDING WORDS

I used to get calls from telemarketers
who asked how I made any money in poetry.
I used to tell the more ignorant sounding
ones that I gave words to what people felt,
but could not say.

I suppose that sounded reasonable enough,
or so they said, but inside I was laughing,
for they had misread my business name from
their teleprompters and cue cards.
it was pottery I made, not poetry,
but maybe that is also a form of poetry—
a kind of handmade Haiku
for those without hands that could make such things.

And maybe there is a lesson there—
a truth that resounds in all things.
For a poet gives voice to those who feel deeply
but struggle to find the words to express.

A plumber cleans drains no one wants to touch.
A dentist repairs teeth no patient can fix on their own.
A doctor heals.
A mother loves.
A baker bakes.
A fisherman catches.
A carpenter builds.
A fireman extinguishes.
A seamstress sews.
And a potter plays in the mud,
making poetry with his hands.

And all these things are poetry to me—
words that sometimes rhyme, but don't have to
as they flow from the hands and hearts
of the poet-doers.

VITAMIN D

Electric Beach, the sign read
and I thought to myself how sad
it must be to have a beach
with only a plugged-in sun;

perhaps a giant sand box
with murals on the wall of
stagnant waves, the recorded sounds
of gulls and surf on a looping tape.

And over there, near the mural
where brightly colored lobsters
are painted close to where the
sandbox meets the wall,

are two flirtatious teenagers,
a tanned young man, and his female companion
in a skimpy bikini, playing that game
with paddle and ball, not concerned about
keeping score, as if the game had no way of scoring at all.

And the longer you stay,
playing in the sand under that
plugged in sun, the more you
start to realize that you've heard

that song of the gulls before—that high pitched screech that
could only mean he has spotted a sand crab,
or the unattended scrap of sandwich
next to your beach towel.

After a while, I would imagine that you have to begin
wondering what this place looks like at night, after they have
unplugged the sun, and turned off the recorded sound of the beach,
so very far away from the real beach.

I have to believe you would feel silly if you stayed,
buried up to your neck in the sandbox, waiting for them
to turn on the electric sun so you could begin a new day at the
Electric Beach, thinking there has to be an easier way to get
A daily dose of Vitamin D.

TEN MINUTE SEGMENTS

If I could divide my life
into ten minute intervals,
I feel quite certain I might
be able to accomplish everything.

Ten minutes for breakfast.
Ten minutes for bidding the kids farewell.
Ten minutes to shower, shave and dress.
Ten minutes to look at the paper.

Ten minutes to clean up the messes of yesterday.
Ten minutes to think about my place
in the universe before jumping into
the chores of the new day—

perhaps write a new poem about
the need for just one more ten minute segment
in which I could write a thank you note
without feeling stressed that I was starving

another ten minute segment of its proper attention
or maybe to go for a ten minute walk
to relieve the stress when too many
ten minutes segments plan a sneak attack

which would of course require another ten minute segment
to beat them off and clean up the mess they leave behind—
those frisky, unthoughtful segments who don't
let me live my life.

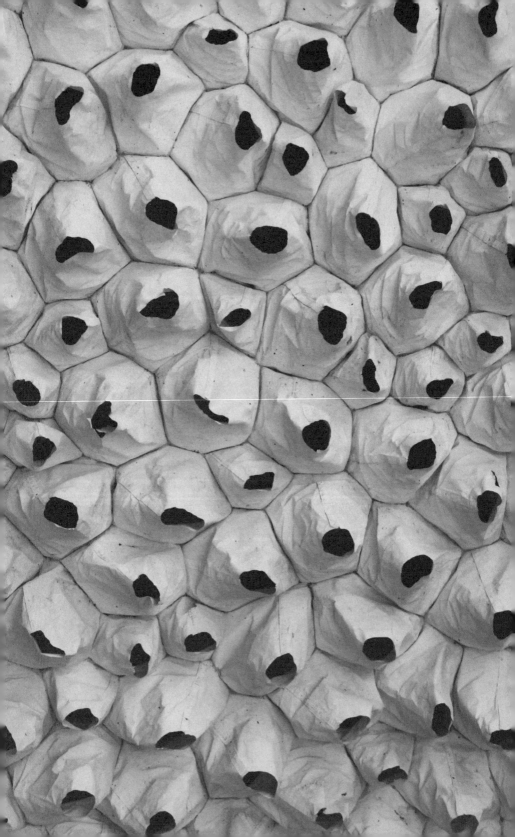

WORTHY OF HONEY

It was only a heel—
and a thin one at that.
She said she already
had enough bread crumbs
for the stuffing.

I considered saving it
for the birds,
but the birds have
mostly gone now, eating bread
somewhere in the southern hemisphere.

So there it sat
on the cold counter
while it's fatter brother
baked in the inferno
where no fork dare wander.

But as its aroma filled my nose
I remembered that two is always better
than one, and despite its anorexic status
I decided it was still
worthy of honey.

WORDS THAT RHYME

These words don't even rhyme,
he said, pointing to the words
at the end of the first two lines
on the first page of my
latest book of collected poems.

Do they need to? I asked,
from my seat behind a table
at the bookstore
and he looked at me with
dark eyes that poked out from
under his Stetson, as if to
ask if I had been born yesterday.

Can you really call yourself a poet then?
he asked, as all the
eyes in the entire bookstore
turned to witness my answer.

I'd like to think I can, I responded.
He slid the book across the table.
I've been looking as I waited here in line,
and I have yet to see even one
decent example of poetry that rhymes,
he said, his voice rising.

And I knew at that moment
that any answer I had given in
the past to explain the hows
and whys of my work would not
be accepted by this man's man
who believed that poetry had to rhyme.

It's a different kind of poetry,
I said out of desperation,
trying to plug the hole his words had
made in my pleasure ship before it
could take on any more water.

And it's good, a woman said, behind
him, adding wadding to my plug.
It's poetry that doesn't have to rhyme
a man said from behind the woman,
and I could feel as the ship began to right itself.

There are poems that rhyme
on the second floor, in the kids section,
a bespectacled employee added,
pointing to the escalators.

He tipped his Stetson and walked away
and I was sad to think of his poor wife
at home on the couch, anxiously awaiting
his return from the bookstore
with my latest book of collected poems,
but then I decided she had bigger fish to fry.

JUAB COUNTY

I read in the paper this morning
a story about a man from Juab County,
and though I have lived in this state
most of my life, I couldn't for the
life of me remember where Juab County is.

You might think I would know better,
after all, there are only twenty-six*
counties in Utah, the same number of letters
in the Alphabet, and I almost never forget
that the letter R is right next to the letter S;

Or that the letter P is the last letter
of the name of Ella Menopee,
who I assume must be the daughter of the
man who invented the Alphabet, and wanted
to create a tribute to his favorite daughter
who was lost in an avalanche of snarky words
that begin with Q, with their nearly always obligatory
second letter, U, that makes such words possible.

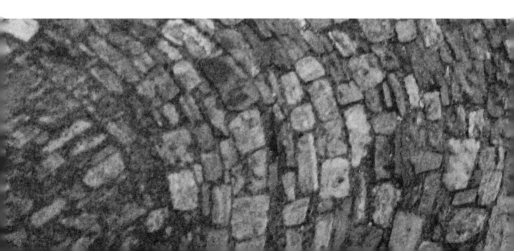

But still I wonder about Juab County,
and how, so many years ago, when there were still
counties to be named, the Jews sat down to breakfast
with the Arabs, each on their own side of the table,
somewhere in Utah, in a county without a name,
to talk peace throughout the day, until late into the evening
when it was decided they would bury their weapons of war
and become brothers, acknowledging their shared lineage
and their common fathers, so many generations ago
when handmaidens were more common and people were
more willing to trade inheritances for bowls of porridge.

And I am grateful and proud that somewhere,
in my great state of Utah, the peace process began,
and together, the Jews and the Arabs formed
the great County of Juab as a beacon of hope to the world,
that the distant cousins of mortal enemies could come together
for at least one day and share breakfast,
perhaps bran muffins and tasty drinking chocolate among other delectables,
and then spread out from that epicenter of Brotherly Love,
to create peace and prosperity around the world.

*Upon closer examination, Utah actually has 29 counties, but whose counting?

SELECTIVE INTERPRETATION

I forgot to bring the
laundry basket **upstairs**
with me, she said as she
stripped off her night clothes
to get into the **SHOWER**.

I realized at that moment that
we have been married
LONG ENOUGH for me to know what
she meant—that it did not mean
that I should sit patiently
at the **bottom** of the stairs

waiting for her to stumble down
in a naked *flight*, dripping wet,
to retrieve her **UNDERWEAR**.

No, it meant that while she
was in the shower, I should
bring up the basket,
and put her clothes away,
and **lay out** her underwear.

But even though
we have been married
more than fifteen years,
I still FANTASIZE about her
shambling down the stairs,
naked and dripping wet to
retrieve the basket.

So this morning
I have decided
to sit,
and eat my granola,
and wait for the *show*.

THE OPTIMIST

I'm feeling pretty good,
he told me with a transparent smile,
and I knew he was only being optimistic—

trying to forget
that his shoulder was disintegrating,
his hip, riddled and pocked with disease,
and the skin on his legs was covered with those
itchy spots that showed up last week
after he started the new medication.

His eyes were dark,
his gut was bloated,
his tongue and teeth
were black from morphine.

His hair was falling out,
his grip was growing weak,
and he had recently lost control
of his bodily functions.

His kidneys were aching,
his liver was shutting down,
he hadn't had a decent bowel
movement since last Friday.

But there he sat,
smiling with those
morphine blackened teeth,
grateful to have one more day
of living and loving.

ODE TO SILENCE

On quiet mornings like this
when the kids have left for
school and my wife is gone,
running carpool,

I cannot help but enjoy the
quiet house with only the sound
of the clock ticking and the
purr of the furnace.

And Oh, the thoughts
this silence breeds!
A veritable garden with flowers of all
colors, popping up before my eyes,

anxious to live, and breathe, and see
a new day that had not yet been
complicated with the pressures of work,
and time, and the endless motion of the sun.

And I have to believe,
on days like today, that this
is the best time of the day,
when silence is rich, and smart, and nourishing

filling my soul with hope,
and power as I watch the sun
carve its way through
the charcoal sky, painting sparkles

on the jar in the window, filled
with last year's harvest of sea shells,
gleaned from the beaches during
morning walks, searching for silence

and finding instead, the song of the ocean,
and these colorful reminders of joy,
and the subtle work of creation
which continues everyday, waiting patiently
for someone to notice the
beautiful fruits of silence and solitude.

WISDOM

I asked a dying man if he
had any bits of wisdom he
might impart to a young man
seeking such stuff.

He thought for a moment
before he looked up brightly.
"Don't shoot unless you have to?"
he said without conviction,
almost questioning the
truth he had just spoken.

But I had to admit the
wisdom was good, and must
have come from somewhere
deep within, leaving me to wonder
what kind of a life he had lived
in his younger years, so long ago,
before the West was won.

But as I looked at him now, so docile,
so demure, strapped to his wheelchair
to keep his body from slouching,
I couldn't help but notice
how his trigger finger was ready
and his disheveled hair
showed the telltale signs of the pistol
that must be cached beneath his pillow.

LOW FAT

It's low fat, she said as she reached
for her third helping of a
CHOCOLATE bar whose fine print
suggested there were ten servings
divided somehow equally in its
segmented **body**.

And I found myself wondering what
it was that made things low fat,
if the portion **SIZES** were
just cut in half or if, before
it left the factory, a priest said
a *prayer* over it, forbidding it

to add poundage to the hips and
thighs and **butt-oxes** of those
who consumed it, or maybe it
meant only that this low fat bar
was stripped of FLAVOR, making it so
no human would want to consume it.

But as I watched her **consume** yet another
of those ten servings somehow crammed into
eight ounces of *brown happiness*,
another thought arose.

How we are all being duped into the notion
of low fat which likely only means that the fat
has somehow been scientifically modified to **sink**
lower than normal, settling into the
calves, the ankles, the TOES

where it can all be *hidden* away by thick **socks**
and high-topped sneakers as it continues
to fool the consumers into believing there
are ten servings in an eight ounce bar of chocolate
when really, there is only **ONE**.

OTHER FRUIT

If you just stare out the window,
the answer will come to you, he told me.
So I tried it, but no answers came;
unless you call the woman who walks
by every morning with her too-tight yoga pants
an answer.

Nor do I believe it was the dog
who left its gift on the neighbor's
lawn while its human, oblivious, talked
on the phone to an unseen lover,
with hands and gestures she surely couldn't see.

Perhaps it was the leaves that fell one
by one until the wind came and tickled
the branches until it gave in
and relinquished more than I could count.

Perhaps it was the taxi driver who waited
impatiently for the girl across the street
who was rumored to have wrapped her
car around a telephone pole one night
after that party, losing her license.

It could be the flock of starlings
that flew in to glean the last of the
wild grapes from the hibernating vine
before flying off again is search of other fruits.

Or maybe it was the three boys
who walked quickly away from
the high school, looking like they
had something to hide.

It could have been the mailman,
or the plumber, or the girl
from Meals on Wheels who brings
Mrs. Jacobs her daily bread.

I'm still not sure what the answer is,
and that's okay, because as I
sat quietly and looked out on the world
I forgot the very question I had asked.

THE TRUTH IN THE SHADOW

If I wrote a poem every morning
before breakfast, I thought to myself,
I would have more than three hundred
poems by the end of the year—
as I am sometimes known to skip breakfast.

So I jotted down some prose while
my tea became cold and my granola, soggy.
And the ideas poured out of me
with each turn of my head;
for I saw that all the world is poetry.

And though there were few things that
rhymed with peppermint, or marmalade,
or even granola, I could see poetry in everything
from the reflection on the toaster to the bouquet
in the window that painted shadows across
the stone countertops and stainless sink.

Which led me to wonder if this was not the way
God intended it when he created the stone
that would become my countertop,
or the flowers that would be in my window
to paint shadows, or the shadow itself…

For surely God must be a poet,
breathing life and beauty
into all creation so those who stop
to see, to hear, to smell, to taste, to touch,

to experience this beauty might know
there is more to life than
rushing from place to place,
burdened, unduly, by the
wingless flight of the sun.

FLYING LESSONS

It's kind of like flying,
I told him as we stood
on top of the tower
and looked out over
the valley, and the one
after that, and the one
after that, too.

Dad, you can put your
arms down now.
You're embarrassing me.

No, this is the part that makes
you feel like your flying;
to lift your wings and feel
the wind carry you away.

Your feet are still
on the ground, Dad,
he said, making that sound
teenagers make when you
fear they might be struggling
to breathe.

But somehow I knew as I flew away
on the East wind that he would
someday bring his own son here
and pretend that he too was a bird.

ALCHEMY IN MOTION

The cherries have come on—
another bumper crop of urban fruit

seeming to have been perfectly timed
once again for the hatchlings

who have just taken
to wing in the last week,

their breasts growing more red with
each heist as they learn from

their parents the crafty art of turning
crimson fruit into white waste,

retaining the color in their breast feathers
which they proudly flaunt

as they make their way
from tree to tree.

VACATION

The corner was empty—
that place at the end of
the off ramp where
the man always stands
with his cardboard sign.

For months he has stood there
with his backpack and
his handwritten declaration of
homelessness
staking claim to his corner of asphalt.

And I am ashamed to admit
there have been many times
when I have imagined him
folding up his sign at the end
of the day, and driving to his home
in the suburbs where he lives with his
wife and kids, in his tax free house,
paid for by the kindness of strangers.

I heard once, a story of a man
who owned a yacht on Balboa Island
and was heard to say he made his
money working six months a year on a
premium piece of asphalt somewhere.
I don't know if it's true.

But the empty street corner is there
and it bothers me that
no one has taken his place.
You would think that such a corner is
prime real estate, with thousands of cars
coming and going throughout the day.

But then I pass another corner
where men and women often stand
with cardboard signs and sad faces,
and it too is empty.

And I can't help but imagine a
yacht filled with grubby looking people,
raising a glass to another good year
and that incredible corner that provided
them with enough money to enjoy a hard
earned vacation from their labors.

WATCHING MELONS

What would you do if you weren't a potter?
she asked me,

and I didn't have to think about it
very long to come up with an answer.

I would string words together to make
stories and poems, I told her.

But what if there weren't any pens or paper,
and no one read books, she asked.

And I told her that such a world
would be a tough place to live.

But still she pressed me so I told her about the men
in Turkey whose only job is to watch the melons grow.

She smiled, and somehow I knew at that moment
exactly what she was thinking—

that she would like to come and visit me on the weekends
in my little bamboo hut overlooking the melon patch

and help me watch the melons grow while I wrote
poetry about those poor people in the city

who eat the melons without ever knowing the men
who watched them grow, and their daughters

who will go anywhere to sit down next to their daddies
and watch the sun set over the melon fields.

THE ALARM

The rooster called my name this morning,
waking me from a shallow slumber.

There are clouds in the next valley over,
he told me incessantly,

speaking of the captive remnants
of last night's storm

that chased away the fireflies
and silenced the song of the crickets.

So I rose from my bed
in the soft morning light

and walked outside to find my laundry
still hanging on the line,

far wetter than it had been
when I hung it there before sunset.

But the rooster called my name again,
distracting me from my soggy laundry,

calling me to witness the death
of the clouds as they grew wispy,

chased away by the gathering breeze
and the rising sun.

I told you so, he called out again,
smiling as only a proud rooster can.

And the last clouds faded
as the new day was born,

leaving me grateful I hadn't slept too long
and missed the magic of its glorious debut.

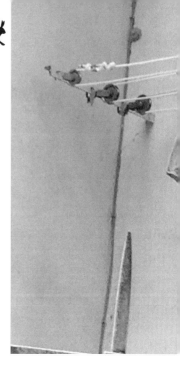

THE REVOLUTION OF LIVING

The laundry was nearly dry when you
asked me for your favorite shirt,
and the dishes had only
just been washed when we
pulled them from the rack
and used them again.
The bedroom was neat and tidy
for about ten minutes before
you came up for bed,
leaving your clothes
strewn across the floor.
And this morning,
the bread was freshly baked,
the milk had just been bought,
and the day was brand new
before you came downstairs
and used it all up—living.

RENT-A-FAMILY

Your phone call was
alarming at first, then
it became amusing
as I thought about it;
your invitation to gather

with a bunch of strangers—
children, siblings, maybe even parents
of your new girlfriend, I forget her name,
whom we met just that once,
almost by accident.

Of course, that was more than
six months ago, and who knows
what has happened in your life
since then, as there have been
no calls, no cards, no love.

Which is why this invitation
to gather with strangers
and build gingerbread houses
seems so odd, cold, but strangely normal
as I contemplate the bygone years,

so full of neglect, abuse, non-understanding.
So I suggest a business model
where parents who have struggled, or not,
for years to be real parents
can rent a family to show off

to their newly-found love—
a family of actors who do not
know the history and will
be whatever you pay them to be;
without baggage, without sorrow; without truth

about how the family has really been
under your direction and neglect,
who do not know about those
three years you sat in front of
the television watching Perry Mason reruns

while the family slid further into
debt, or the times your voice and
words drove us all away from the
house for weeks on end after
that letter arrived from the I.R.S.

And though your invitation sounded sincere,
and though I would like nothing more
than to have a real family, the history we share
makes me believe you would be better off
spending the money to rent a family.

MASTERS OF STRATEGIC COMMUNICATION

The advertisement for the new course
of study conjured up all sorts of ideas,
leaving me wondering what it might be
like to learn to interface in such a way
that through strategy one might
gain the upper hand over ones
foes and friends alike.

Communicating in such a way as to
create an unfair playing field:
a war fought with secret weapons
or a game of chess where you know
by some strategic means the next
five plays your opponent will make.

I'm certain I would be intimidated
speaking to one who held a such a degree,
wondering if he was really listening at all
or simply waiting for me to inadvertently

step into his well-placed snare,
exposing my Achilles Heel,
whereby he might, through strategy, take
advantage of my weakness and mess up my whole day.

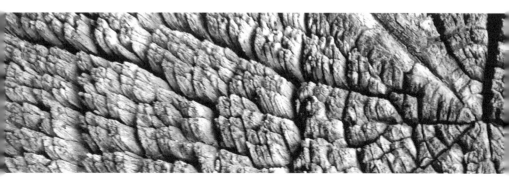

Which leads me to wonder who
came up with this course of study;
perhaps a professor of normal communications
who began taking steroids and decided

regular, polite, friendly communication
was no longer good enough and lacked
an element of surprise and competition,
a way to win, if you will,

creating instead a new set of rules and
dialogual devices wherewith,
after gaining mastery of verbal
sword and cimeter, he might gain supremacy
over all those who dare challenge him.

But despite the threat such a school of thought poses,
I have decided that instead of spending the next
two to four years obtaining the guarded secrets,
my time will likely be better spent learning to listen
and leaving the less important strategy of it all
to those who believe there has to be a winner.

A DECADE EARLY

We'll have to come back in ten years,
I told him as we got back into the car
after looking through the fence,
into the treasure-laden junkyard.

By then, the dog will be dead,
and it's owner too,
and we can take
all the pictures we want.

And as we drove away
he agreed with me
that from sound of the bark
we were at least a decade early.

PUMPKIN PANCAKES

"There is a bus with my name on it,"
he said, "And you never know… "
And I found myself wondering
if people who think like
that should even get out of bed

or if it might be better to stay
beneath the covers and dream
about happy places where there is
no fear, or danger lurking, waiting
to pounce, to rob, to kill.

But in my minds eye, I can see that bus,
driven by a crazed madman
who has been up since Tuesday,
consuming nothing but black
coffee as he drives around town
running people over—on purpose.

I know a woman who
has wished for twenty years
that today would be her last.
And tomorrow when she rises, she will
wish the same, and the next day, and the next.

It's a pity the universe can't
find a way to bring together the
psychotic bus driver and the woman with a death wish;
a sacrifice of sorts to appease the
bus who'll eventually come for each of us.

But today I got up, not thinking
about the bus, or dying, or even the old lady.
I got up to live, and it's been good
so far, making pumpkin pancakes
that helped me remember
there is still so much to live for.

FORGOTTEN PICNICS

Did you bring the picnic?
she asked, looking hopeful.

I'm sure I looked at her funny,
not knowing that was my job.

Of course I should have thought
about bringing something,

I mean, three hours without food
is an awful long time.

And it was hard to
concentrate after that,

wondering what we would eat
for lunch and thinking

about those sandwiches,
nicely packed, in the basket,

cozying up to the apples and drinks,
and those tasty cupcakes,

ready to be taken out for a good time,
but instead left somewhere

between the kitchen and the front door,
dreaming of better days.

A Toast to a Sunday Afternoon of Boredom

I wonder if they could have known,
those Chinese brothers
whose last name has been forever
lost to history,
how that game they invented
out of boredom on their mother's
dining room table
could spread across the world
in such a flurry, sweeping up
men and women, boys and girls
who would spend so many hours
trying to improve their skills at
this challenging sport of
tit for tat, yin and yang, back and forth;
or how their paddles could have
evolved from their crudely shaped
cutting boards into the standard shape
so common today.
And so I raise a toast to these
brothers whose surname
I wish I knew,
long live Ping,
and his creative brother, Pong!

A SEED OF HOPE

I have held onto one piece of HOPE
for many years, he told me,
emotion hanging on his words.

And when he described it, I could see
why that one piece of hope had KEPT
him going, that small window on eternity.

And though that window had been open
for only *seconds*, it had given him two decades
of hope, growing dimmer with each PASSING

year as he had researched the elements of **grief**,
recognizing that his vision may have been little more
than a side effect of a **BROKEN HEART.**

And so each year, the *light* of his hope diminished;
its power WEAKENED by doubt, one small piece
at a time until only a **sliver** of hope remained.

That hope that might have grown had the seed
landed in FERTILE soil had rather withered and died,
choked by the briars of doubt before it could bloom.

But still the memory, however distant, remained,
lying DORMANT, waiting with patience, continuing
its pure *goodness*, hoping beyond hope

that it might **sprout** once more, and grow,
and become something more than a seed;
a tiny, PRECIOUS GIFT that remained UNOPENED,
unexamined, unaccessed; starved of its potential to
NOURISH, to offer refuge, to bear fruit.

WISHES

Be careful
what you wish for,
he used to tell me,

and in the chaos of those moments
I don't think I could have possibly
understood him.

But now, as I find myself somehow missing
those crazy, hysteric, manic times when
all the world was in commotion,

I'm beginning to understand
what he was trying to tell me—
to savor those times

when all it takes is
his goofy smile and her tiny voice
to set the world right.

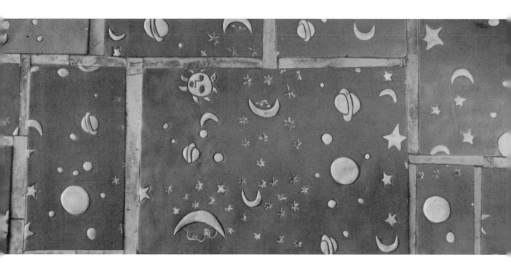

ACCEPTABLE IGNORANCE

How big does a cloud
have to be before it can
have RAIN inside of it?
she asked.

And it made me wonder if
her question was *really* about clouds
or, if I had an answer for this one,
where her questions would ever stop.

But I didn't want to
ADMIT I didn't know,
so I told her that a cloud had to be
at least as big as a barn.

A big barn or a small barn? she asked
after a moment's thought and I decided
then and there to admit I didn't know,
FEARING my ignorance would cause her to lose respect.

But to my surprise,
for the very first time in our *long history*
of important QUESTIONS and impossible answers,
that seemed to be **good enough** for her.

ABSENCE IN PRESENCE

You missed it!
The walk in the Alps at twilight
as the wind pushed the smoky clouds
through the verdant canyon,
and the sliver of the moon smiled down
on the waterfall that tumbled a thousand feet
over the face of the cliff;
the same color as the glacier that fed it,
somewhere up there, beyond view.

While you checked your Instagram
to see how many friends liked your post,
so far away, on the other side of the world,
you missed this sheer awesomeness,
this, that is right before you, this, the giant
pieces of slate that form the roof of all the
buildings in the valley, speckled with centuries
of lichen, each stone certainly
weighing more than yourself.

You also missed the yellow wild flowers
that climb the hill by the ski slope,
and the jet trail that burns hot pink
above the horizon.

And while I'm thinking about it,
you missed the sweet smell on the wind
and the colorful flowers that adorned
the windows and the bridge and the
carved out logs that formed planters.
You missed sitting on the stone wall
and watching the lady across the river
bring in her laundry.

While you worried if anyone would comment
on the twentieth selfie you have posted with
your tongue stuck out, you missed it all—
and I—I missed you, seeing this place
through your eyes too for the first and last
time the sun ever will rise and set on this day.

THE SLOW WAY

We could have stopped thirty kilometers back,
back at the town whose name I could not pronounce,

but instead, we drove on, looking for something more
than that awful room they offered us at eighty-five euros

just after we had declined to pay the fifty euros to the
woman at the toll booth which could have shaved

an hour off the trip, a route that would prove once again
that man, with his grit and intellect can conquer nature

by drilling a hole through the middle of her
without recognizing all that is missed in the quicker passage;

the winding roads and narrow streets,
passing houses built before Columbus sailed from Spain.

We would have missed the fromagerie,
and the geraniums that overflow the boxes outside

the window of our rented room on the top floor
that offers a commanding view of the valley

and the towering cliffs with their jagged teeth that
lunge at the horizon, their glaciers crying tears of joy

that cascade slowly, draping the mountain in green carpet
until combining in the clear river whose yodels echo

off the walls as I strain my ears to understand,
leaving me feeling grateful that we took the slow way.

AGAIN TO PING AND PONG

Dad, I want a copy of that Ping Pong Poem,
he told me, just a couple of nights
after I first shared it with him.

And I started feeling happy, like I was finally
making progress with helping my son to open
his mind and heart to new ideas.

Poets are so weird, he said next,
which only slightly deflated my happiness,
knowing I really couldn't argue.

But still I was happy to have, at long last,
written a poem that caught my son's attention,
something he recalled with laughter, even days later.

So once again I raise a toast
to Ping, and his creative,
but slightly weird brother, Pong.

NO REMORSE

We would have shared
one of the FRESH pastries
I brought home this morning
from the **bakery** in the village
that had just opened for
business when I walked by
after taking pictures of the sunrise,
but they tasted so GOOD with the
peppermint tea that we couldn't
resist eating them all by **ourselves**,
hoping that in your visit
to the Land of Nod,
you would NOT miss them.

I would tell you that we will
share with you TOMORROW,
but I hate breaking promises.

THE VALUE OF LAUGHTER

Is it hard being married to a weirdo?
I asked her one night after we'd spent
half an hour talking in bed.

There is never an absence of things
to laugh at, she responded.

And I smiled, grateful to be married
to the one woman in the world
who understands me and fuels my fire
with her contagious, sometimes irreverent,
but always sincere laughter.

LIGHT

Hold tight to the soft light of evening; for tomorrow there be rain, or sun, or wind, or noise to distract from that light which offers clarity and tranquil peace.

AFFLICTIONS OF A PART-TIME WRITER

Isn't it strange how some days
the ideas pour out of your head;
gushing waterfalls, making everything
lush and green and fertile;

and then the next day, for no
particular reason, your mind is
the desert— barren, empty,
with only the dust devils to keep
you company with their constant
churning, but going nowhere?

Is it because I slumped on the couch
last night, indulging in internet videos
of people making their debut on
America's Got Talent instead of reading a book?

Or maybe it's because this morning
I read from a stack of quotes from the
founding fathers instead of from that
book of poetry that always paints vivid
pictures in my mind.

Or maybe the muses of poem and thought
have not yet awoken for the day,
secretly planning a sneak attack—
to commence at the exact second
I put my hands to my work.

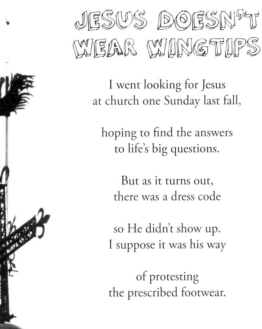

JESUS DOESN'T WEAR WINGTIPS

I went looking for Jesus
at church one Sunday last fall,

hoping to find the answers
to life's big questions.

But as it turns out,
there was a dress code

so He didn't show up.
I suppose it was his way

of protesting
the prescribed footwear.

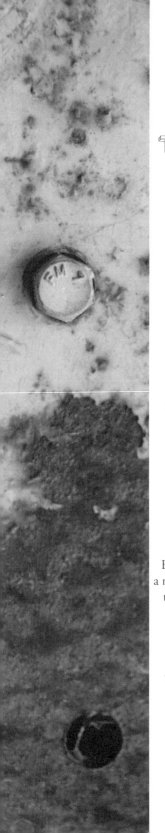

TRADE IN VALUE

It's not much to look at
but it's all I've got,
he told me as he pulled himself
from his old recliner and reached
for his keys.

I've been thinking about trading
it in for a newer one
but they're not offering much
for my make and model.

I knew he was right,
having recently driven past
their bone yards,
filled to overflowing with late models
in a variety of colors and
various shades of decline.

And it left me wondering what
he could possibly get for his
ol' jalopy, his tires worn down
and his headlights smashed in,
fenders held on with bailing wire;

But I followed him, knowing he'd need
a ride home; his muffler making sparks on
the pavement as he drove slowly down
the lane with an optimistic smile
on his face to the dealer at the
end of the road,
hoping he might overlook
the faded paint and the rusty bumper.

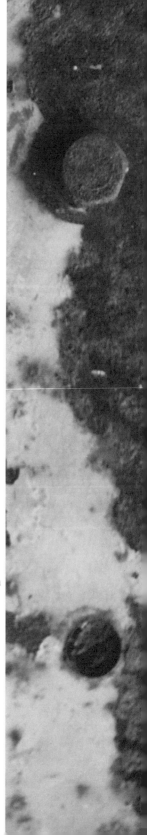

STRETCH

How far can you stretch?
she asked as she stood
at the foot of our bed,
reaching for my hyper-ticklish toes
which I had swung up near her pillow,
trying to avoid the attack.

Not far enough, I replied
pulling back, out of reach
of her menacing fingers.

But her question left me wondering
how far I could stretch—should stretching
suddenly become necessary, and if it might
be sufficient to avoid discomfort, and tickles,
or whatever the case may be.

And so I decided right then and there
that is was time to take those contortionist
classes through community education
that I've always considered but never
made the time for.

STUDIO VISIT

I visited a painter's studio this afternoon,
downtown in a building that was built
before electricity was common.

We traded a bunch of pottery that his wife
picked out for a nice, small painting of
a glass half full.

It got me thinking about art and painting
and the importance of surrounding oneself
with beauty and creativity
in order for the muses to speak.

It has been close to fifteen years since
I was last in that building, back when I used
to paint, back before the moths ate
the hair off my brushes.

For the past ten years I have been buying
new brushes, and canvases, and even tubes
of paint, waiting, thinking, planning on getting
back into it, hoping there might come a time
when I can justify dipping my brushes
back into the color.

But today, when I was hit in the nose with the
scent of turpentine, my fingers began to itch
with creativity, with the desire to paint clouds
and still lifes, and chum around again with painters
and artists and spend long mornings with
other creative folks, eating breakfast at Lamb's Grill.

And come home feeling excited, inspired, driven, smart,
wanting to open that old bottle of turpentine,
squeeze out a line of paint, and create for myself
a new world.

ODE TO GINGER ALE

O, that **ROYAL** nectar,
that golden juice of the ginger root
so delightfully **wedded** with sugar
and bubbling fizzy water

that ti**ck**les the nose before
delighting the **TONGUE** with its
spicy, mystical effervescence!

O, how I wish *I* had invented you
and learned to bottle you up
in all your v a r i e t i e s , preserved
in the finest of jeweled bottles,

purest AMBER, sparkling as if
infused with the sun itself.
How glad I am that you came
into my life and brought me
such splendid happiness.

SILENCIO

SHHHHHHHHH! Silencio!
The loudspeaker echoed
off the tall, ancient walls
of that sacred space
built so long ago,
before tourists, before silence
had to be sought out,
before cameras and high heels,
back when silence came naturally
to this space for worship,
when the people came
to pray and commune—
not to wait in long lines
to gawk at the dome—
so high above, and the windows,
and the marble floors;
exponentially more people
on a Wednesday afternoon than
ever for a Sunday mass;
people who have come looking
for ancient beauty,
but not the ancient silence
that was produced when
man first conceived of placing
stone upon stone,
searching for
a place to call holy.

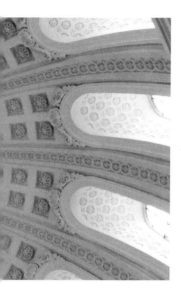

SHOULDER PATROL

Excuse me, Miss,
he said as she walked through
the door of the cathedral,
but your dress in not allowed.

He pointed to her shoulders
which were bare
except for the strap which
held up her top.

You will have to
purchase a covering
if you want
to come in.

She grimaced,
looking down
at her
beautiful dress.

He handed her the yellow,
plastic poncho
and took
her money

And I had to admit I was grateful
that I didn't have to wear
a silly poncho to approach
the altar of God.

4 THINGS

Taking pictures in Europe
falls into four categories,
I explained to him.

1. Doors
2. Windows
3. Bikes
4. Cows.

Is that all? he asked.

Well, no, of course not,
but the sun doesn't shine
that often, and I've found
you're a lot less disappointed
if you can be happy
with those four things.

CICADA INTERLUDE

There is both a *song*
and a rhythm to their music,
those bugs so high in the **TREES**,
singing something about
how unbearably HOT the day is,
asking why they waited
s e v e n t e e n y e a r s to hatch from
the ground on a day like this
which must be similar
to the one that inspired **Dante**
to write his INFERNO.

And perhaps they will record
in their DNA
a song for the **underworld**
which might inspire their progeny
to come again in,
SEVENTEEN years time,
on a glorious day in S p r i n g .

LINGER LONGER

I wonder what happens in the morning,
what bit of magic takes place, early
when I am in the shower, so full of thoughts,
of words, of great ideas—so full of poetry.

Those thoughts continue to linger while I
shave and put on my deodorant,
and work up a lather on my teeth,
but by the time I pull on my clothes,
the words are gone, the magic—evaporated,
mirages burned off in the
heat and pressure of day.

So maybe I need to spend more time **naked** …
exposed, with nothing but a thin piece
of glass, separating me from the world,
the cold, the eyes and ears of criticism.

What is about the rawness of morning
that inspires such creative goodness,
such altruism of vocabulary,
such generosity of dreams and vision,
and abundance of happy thoughts?

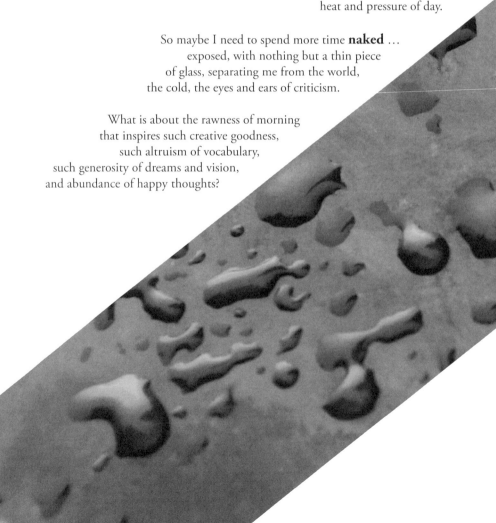

Perhaps it would be better if
I could set up my office in the comforting womb
of my shower and tempt those thoughts to linger
indefinitely, not to be chased off by the
malevolent forces of work, of day, of life.

Forces who are quick to rob the
precious moments, eager to blot out
the morning light with
the gray, leaden clouds of time.

Tomorrow, or maybe the next day,
I will stay in that creative moment
a little longer and allow myself
to be showered by that creative power of morning,
those golden moments before
the cares of day awake.

MONSOON @ 5 AM

It was only a ten minute monsoon
that woke me an hour before sunrise—

a years worth of rain falling at once
overflowing the gutters with such force

that I'm sure it upset the landscaping,
carrying away small rocks and bushels of mulch,

the same way it might on the savannah,
waking the frogs that have been dormant since last year,

encrusted deep within the parched earth
waiting patiently for this rare moment

when water stacks up in puddles,
offering a blink of lush vibrancy,

spawning new life in an otherwise
harsh, thirsty, dehydrated landscape

which caused me to put pen to paper
and hour before sunrise and write something

that will help me to remember the sound
of the rain when the sun scorched earth

once again encrusts my frog brain
with the quicksand of day.

CONVERSATION AT THE END OF THE DAY

Do you want to make out? I asked.
Sure, she responded, do you?
Actually … no. I was really just feeling
tired and couldn't think of anything
better to say.
You're weird, she told me,
and I quickly decided it was better to agree
as I rolled over and turned out the light.

LISTENING

The incessant call of an unseen bird to its mate.
The bark of a frog.
The purr of the tires on the distant highway.

The quick flutter of a bee's wings.
The quivering hum of the breeze as it passes
through the branches and leaves.

The rattle of the grasshoppers wings.
The startling caw of a crow.
The high pitched buzz of the menacing flies.

The melodious squeal of a child's laugh.
The tiny chirp of the humming birds.
The rattled beat of the desert quail.

The sound of me breathing, listening to the
morning sounds, waiting patiently, silently,
for the inspiration to come.

Late Night Lamentations

I'll have to pay for this in the morning,
I told myself as I started my fourth poem
since midnight when the moon was shining
so brightly through my window that
I couldn't sleep, which is perhaps one of the
biggest tragedies of mortality—the frailty
of the human form that drags on us,
weighing down that weightless part of us—
that part that knows no fatigue, or limits,
or road blocks to becoming and experiencing,
without the tragedy that befalls our bodies
when they become drunk with slumber;
hibernation caves for the growling bear
who would like to attack the new day,
but holds back only out of fear
of waking the neighbors.

A SUMMER POEM

There is poetry hiding in the tall grass,
but there is also poetry in the freshly shorn grass
with the scents of summer wafting about
on the whispered breeze, tickling the leaves
on the tallest branches.

There is poetry that floats about the yard
on the fine strands of spider silk,
reflecting the yellow sun.

There is poetry in the erratic flight
of the white butterfly that flutters about
with no goal in sight.

There is poetry in the song of the birds,
and the nap I slipped into while writing
this poem on a summer afternoon.

And I woke to find that all the world is a poem,
touched on all sides by the ballad-rich air, whispering songs
in the ears of those who choose to breathe it in.

THE TRUTH ABOUT CHEESE

I woke this morning to **find** my cheese
in the SINK, exiled from the fridge
because of its tiny specks of green.

And this is just to say that I was **angry**,
knowing that with very little effort
the OFFENSIVE spots could be so easily scraped away
and the precious cheese p r e s e r v e d —
back in the fridge.

I spent the day **brooding**, wondering if
the time has arrived for ME to get my own
fridge where my cheese
and other fine morsels of happiness

might be ***cached*** without the threat
of deportation and annihilation when
found bearing INCRIMINATING blemishes.

Will you do the same with me
when I have lived beyond my **prime**,
and my hair begins to fall out,
and my walks **turns** to a shuffle?

Will I wake one morning to FIND myself
in the sink, READY to be tossed out
to make room for the younger, less mature
cheeses who are less offensive and, oh, so less f l a v o r f u l ?

PRACTICE

The long, dusty road to perfection is surely
pocked with the potholes of practice,
I thought to myself as I rolled out of bed,
having tried desperately to practice sleeping in.

Then I practiced eating a sensible breakfast
while concurrently practicing poetry
in an effort to try to slow down;
a practice of meditation, searching for the
ever-ambiguous zen, while also practicing my faith
in the spirit that comes to me
in words and thoughts and song.

I went to the studio
and practiced my art, practiced creation,
practiced the story telling of my hands.
I practiced more faith, believing people
will come and buy my wares.

I practiced positive thought throughout the day
thinking about all the things I could be doing
on one of the last cloudless days of fall.
I practiced determination when
the distracting characters,
words, and literary ideas
hovered above me like a hawk,
waiting for a mouse
to appear in the grass below.

I practiced cleanliness, but I did not succeed,
so I practiced procrastination instead
before practicing restraint—not swearing when the day
was only half as productive as I hoped.
I practiced gratitude as I ate my dinner.
I practiced love as my family sat near me,
distracted by the thoughts, that tomorrow, when I rise,
I will try to do better as I practice away another day
on this long and dusty road to that ever-elusive destination
called Perfection.

BLOWING SMOKE

How great would it be if we could
take every negative emotion
and drop it into a giant hand-cranked mill
that would mix them up with herbs and spices
and other bits of happiness to produce
succulent sausages that bore no resemblance
to the bitter sentiments we once held onto?

And instead of cursing and kicking
and carrying on, we could invite
our neighbors and friends to come for a visit,
to drop their own burdensome emotions
into the mill at the front door,
giving the ol' crank a few turns
before wandering out to the backyard
where people are loafing about congenially,
telling jokes and swapping tales
as the succulent sausages are grilled,
blowing a lovely aroma across the neighborhood,
making the whole town consider having a
barbecue of their own.

JEALOUS LOVER

I really should invest in some of that
waterproof paper I thought to myself
as I stood under the shower,
thinking of new poems;

you know, the kind that scuba divers
use to record the fish they see
or the poems that are inspired by their
underwater excursions,

but then I would probably spend
way too much time in the shower,
the water turning cold long before I am
done recording my morning thoughts,

before the day becomes complicated with
such things as clothes and appointments
and responsibilities that so selfishly occupy
my mind like a jealous lover,

tearing me away from much more important things,
making me forget the thoughts I had in the shower
when the day was fresh and the muses
danced around me, urging me to stay
in the warm, nourishing womb of morning.

TRADING LIFE

It has been three weeks since I
took the time to write,
spending my time making pots
instead, which I will soon trade
for a handful of sweaty dollars,
crumpled bills, and a swipe of
plastic cards that will somehow
signify that I am successful,
providing for me and my family
another meal, another month
of no worries, a sense of security.

But at what cost?
What have I missed in that time?
Twenty one mornings to sit quietly
and think, and see the many things
I normally miss when the deadlines
loom like icy cornices, waiting to
break loose at any moment and fall,
pushing me further away from that
elusive goal of sitting still,
or laying down and watching,
if only for ten short minutes,
the path of the clouds across the sky
and remember again why it is I trade
my life for a fist full of sweaty dollars.

EASY LIVING?

Whoever said that the living
is easy in the summertime
must have never had
a sunburned stomach,
or more mosquito bites
on his legs than freckles.

He probably never tried to sleep
on a bed in a room that was too hot
to afford such luxuries as a
decent night's sleep.

Maybe he never had to get up
early to mow the lawn before
the grass died in the afternoon sun,
or to run to the pool
before the water evaporated,
making it quite difficult to swim.

No, the living is not so easy,
each breath labored and heavy,
but while the long, hot summer is here,
I suppose it's a good thing to tell the kids.

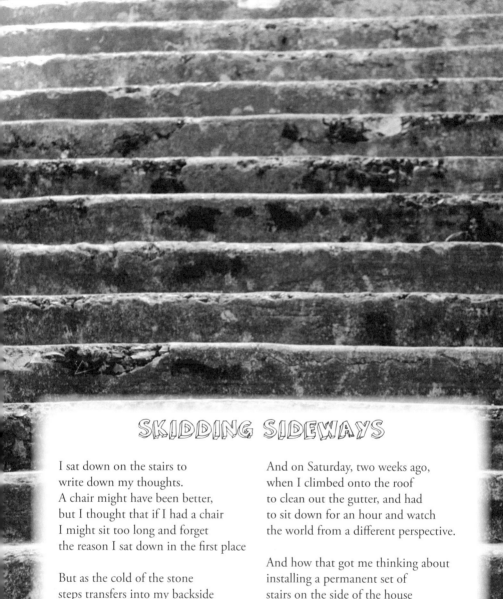

SKIDDING SIDEWAYS

I sat down on the stairs to
write down my thoughts.
A chair might have been better,
but I thought that if I had a chair
I might sit too long and forget
the reason I sat down in the first place

But as the cold of the stone
steps transfers into my backside
I begin to wonder what it was
I wanted to write down
so I would never forget

And that reminded me of Wednesday,
the day of the first snow
when I watched from my window
the cars trying to make their way
up the steep hill, skidding sideways.

And on Saturday, two weeks ago,
when I climbed onto the roof
to clean out the gutter, and had
to sit down for an hour and watch
the world from a different perspective.

And how that got me thinking about
installing a permanent set of
stairs on the side of the house
so I could go up there anytime at all
without fussing with the ladder.

And maybe that's why I'm here,
sitting on this stone step when I
really should be working, but had to
stop and remember what it felt like to
see the world from a very high place.

PACIFIC COAST DREAMS

I dreamt last night of the
Pacific Coast Highway, again;

driving down that scenic byway,
through towns named for gods and kings,

the sparkling sea on my right side
and the homes that could belong

to the aforementioned gods and kings
on my left—heading south.

But I woke this morning, cold,
tired, blue; for I know that outside my window

is no sunlit sea,
no streets named for gods or kings,

but rather darkness, gray smog,
winter without sun to burn off the marine layer—

if we had a marine layer;
wishing beyond reasonable wishes

for a beach day—to have nothing
on my agenda beyond walking

from one end of the beach to the other,
picking up bits of beach glass and sea shells

until the tide pushes me all the way home
to spend another glorious night dreaming

of the sand between my toes
and the sound of the shorebirds,

the smell of the salty brine,
and the millions of sparkles on the sunlit sea.

VAN WINKLE'S HAIR

It was only a short nap—
okay, maybe longer than
it should have been, close to
three hours on a lazy Sunday
afternoon where my body felt
justified in the relief that comes
only after a week of heavy work.

I splashed my face with cold water
and looked into the mirror, surprised
to find my hair had turned gray in
the hours of my siesta like
Rip Van Winkle's nap of twenty years,

leaving me wondering what events
I must have missed as my head
rested all those years on my pillow,
me, too tired to feel or see the rushing
of the years that passed without a sound.

PRACTICAL SOLUTION #419

Just because you're taller that me now
doesn't mean you can put my head in your armpit,
she told him as he stood in the kitchen
before breakfast and hugged his mother.

And I was forced to acknowledge that
he was growing up, so I did the only thing
that made any sense at that moment—
I chased him down and tackled him
on the couch where I drew flowers
on his bare chest with a black marker
until he was laughing once again
like a little kid,
and we all felt much better after that.

HOPES AND PROMISES

I hope we will always be friends,
I told her,
and she promised me we would.
But when you're only ten,
it's hard to make a promise
that is in any way binding,
so I decided to forget about
hopes and promises
and sit back and enjoy our view
of the meadow where the fireflies
mirrored the lights of the stars.

SEARCHING FOR BALANCE

I can't do it,
he told me, looking at
the tall, narrow towers of
loose rocks I had stacked,
one upon the other
in my search for balance
on a Sunday afternoon.

It only takes time,
I assured him. Time and patience.
But he did not hear me,
having ditched his rocks,
he ran off to find a more
exciting kind of balance
of his own.

And as I continued to stack
rock upon rock, I decided that's
the way it should be, finding
balance in our own way,
answers only we can know,
some requiring time and patience,
others justified only by the minds
of those who seek them
without compromise.

A TOO-BRIGHT MOON

I tried to sleep
but the moon was
too bright, coming through
the skylight in the
closet, shining in on
all our clothes, making
me think of that
time in Maui when
I bought that silk
shirt that you thought
looked good on me,
and the time you
wore that dress when
it was still new
to her wedding party
when her brothers put
on those Sumo suits
and wrestled on the
grass, making everyone laugh.
And don't get me
started on those shoes,
both yours and mine
and all the miles
we've walked and danced
and all the places they've
carried us off to,
both near and far.
Which reminds me of
that pretty pottery bowl
on the dresser that
I bought in Philadelphia,
now filled with all
the money left over
from things we bought
which only makes me
wonder why we don't
round things up or
down to the nearest
dollar so we don't
have to have bowls
of coins waiting around
for the kids to
want a Slurpee or
frozen yogurt and have
to earn their treat
by counting change that
has been sitting around
for who knows how
many moons, which leads
me to wonder if,
after all that, the
too-bright moon is
really the reason I'm
still awake?

PREPAID FUNERALS

He was an old friend, both in age and one of my very first—
the man who helped me cross the street on my way
to school each day for seven years with his plastic
stop sign and orange jacket,

but as I stumbled upon his grave this afternoon
it bothered me that the stone which marks
the final resting place of his earthly remains
has been left unfinished.

I attended his graveside service some time back,
representing the thousands of kids he crossed
over more than thirty years of crossing streets.

Clearing away the needles from his grave I recalled
his friendship and kindness and the surprising tears
that came, standing there at his open grave, some time back
on that chilly, fall day …

… or was it a chilly spring day? I know it was chilly—
a definite chill in the air. But his stone offers no help
to my shady memory—the month and day and year
of his death not yet carved into the face of the granite slab

that had been placed at the time of his wife's funeral;
she being the first to go, he had time to get the details
finished up before laying down beside her under the
giant blue spruce; their love now entangled in its roots.

Which leaves me to wonder what happened to the stonemason
who was supposed to finish the work he started;
if he is still waiting to hear of my friend's death, or perhaps
more likely, is laying on a beach somewhere, his mallet and chisel
long forgotten as he soaks up the sun, grateful for the invention of
prepaid funerals.

MUFFLED BY LAUNDRY

I wish I took more time to sit next to my love,
not needing to say anything—

simply listening to the rhythms of my own heart—and hers;
those two rhythms that matter most and are so often muffled

under the piles of laundry that get heaped upon them,
only to be seen and heard at times like this,

when at 35,000 feet on an intercontinental fight,
I have decided that the incessant roar of the engines

provides just enough silence and distraction
from my normal pace for me to finally listen.

THE EASIEST ANSWER

Why are we having Fanta for breakfast?
she asked, and I watched as the children
looked at her with pouty faces as if she
were questioning the frivolous and unnecessary
presence of joy in life itself.

Because we're on vacation!
I replied, surprised by my own words that
generally lean towards more practical answers.

But she nodded, and said no more,
and for the rest of the week
that answer proved to be
the most popular and
oft repeated answer given,
and there was great rejoicing
that such silly questions
could be so easily tempered.

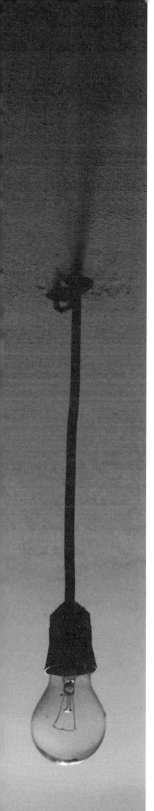

ODE TO SMALL REMINDERS

It only required the reading
of one of Neruda's odes
to common things for me to
realize how ungrateful I have been.

How I have looked past the
beauty in the rug, the salt shaker,
the scissors which bear both curves and
sharp edges, offering the potential
for both comfort and pain.

And as I look around I notice so many
other things I have missed: the lightbulb,
the steering wheel, the pocket knife with
its many fingers and multiple functions.

And don't get me started on the unseen
things that make my life better;
the microwaves, the transmission gears,
the satellites so far above this blue marble,
 sending bits of data at the speed of light.

It all makes me feel ungrateful,
when with each turn, I see things
that add beauty and meaning
to my life everyday, and yet I have never
taken much time to think about;

the cloth that keeps me warm,
the water flowing hot from the tap,
the razor that trims my whiskers,
or the thousands of bees who make the honey
that sweetens my tea.

All of theses things and so many more
pass through my fingers without thought,
without a thank you, without notice,
without an expression of love

until I stop, feeling the gentle tug
of a spider's snare that was set for
much smaller prey, but caught me instead,
causing me to slow down and remember
the significance and beauty of little things.

MY PLACE

Hey, you took **my** place,
he said, returning from
finally putting away his guitar
which he had left in the
MIDDLE of the family room
when he returned from his
lesson, **SO** many hours ago.

When I did NOT move, he lay
down, much has he had before
I insisted he take care
of his guitar, resting his head
on *my* thigh.

Your leg's not as soft as the pillow,
he said, and I decided to be **grateful**
that in his THIRTEEN YEARS he had
come to recognize that things with
bones running though the middle
of them are **inherently** somewhat
harder than the boneless pillow
he had been lazily resting his head
on before I brought to his attention
that his guitar, which we spent
good money on **before** the lessons
even began, was lying, quite forgotten
in the **middle of the floor**, and he was there,
taking up my space on the comfy couch
which I had called dibs on long before
he was even born!

PEACHES

It was the last thing
we did together, she told me.

looking into the pantry,
its shelves lined with dull, dusty bottles

filled with peaches in various
shades of brown, still bearing

the mark of the knife that had so
delicately peeled them.

I couldn't bring myself to eat them, she told me,
emotion thick in the back of her throat.

It was easy to imagine her standing next to him
at the sink so many years before

as they had done so many years before that,
father and daughter,

laying up peaches for those wintry days
when peaches would be hard to come by,

when one could sit down to a bowl
of bright peaches and remember

the day when life had definition,
and love, and companionship,

but as we looked in on them now
the thought of eating brown, mushy fruit

made us both turn up our noses
and recognize it was time to dump the peaches.

OPPORTUNITIES

Why did we wait until the last day
to do this? she asked as we stripped off
our bathing suits and jumped into the pool
before the kids woke up.

I'm not sure, I said, but we really ought to
have taken more opportunity to do this over the years
when we were skinnier and more attractive.

We still have a few good years, she responded,
and I nodded, knowing she was right, but also aware
that there's a mighty big difference between
skinny dippin' and chunky dunkin'.

WAITING ON THE INEVITABLE

Puberty has been good to me,
he announced, as he strutted through
the kitchen, boastfully showing off his
washboard of a bare chest and his
recently acquired armpit hair.

His mother and I were speechless as
we looked at each other, deciding it was
futile to argue with the transformation
that was rather quickly changing
boy into man.

And even though a big part of me
wanted to respond with something that
might keep him humble, I decided to let it go,
knowing life would eventually catch up to him,
and he would need to remember the time
when he had it good.

I NEVER CONSIDERED

the poetry in taking out the garbage
until I did it one Monday morning
dragging the cans to the curb
while the traffic sped by, unaware
of the beauty of that moment
in their rush to arrive.

I almost missed the poetry
as I joined the throng of commuters,
but found it, blatantly apparent in the low
hanging clouds that veiled the mountain tops,
giving privacy to the gods who performed
their secret magic, turning them
from brown to white overnight.

And I wondered how long this has been going on?
—this poetry all around me in the most simple of things.

But a voice in my head whispers back:
poetry is always found in simple things;
the flowers you trample underfoot,
the clouds you tend to ignore,
the trees you so often neglect.

Poetry is everywhere!
the voice continued,
lurking quietly under
the chaos you pile on top of it,
pretending it's fun to be busy.

But look what you have missed!
Look how the trees are dancing,
and the snow is sparkling,
and your life has gathered a thin blanket
of dust, waiting for you to take notice
and come back from being too busy,
to see and hear and recognize the poetry
in everything, hidden just beneath the
chaos you piled upon it,
burying the beauty of the moment
in your race to get on to
much less important things.

FIFTY-NINE CENTS

Seemed like a reasonable price to pay
for a single golden banana.

Of course I remember paying far less
in recent years, like that time
in Philadelphia at the Reading Terminal
when I bought four for a dollar.

Or that time in Miami when they
were only thirty-nine cents a piece,
but then those were mostly green
and never fully ripened.

But I got to wondering what
all goes into the cost of a banana
grown in a distant country.

I suppose it would have to begin with
the cost of the plantation; planting trees,
keeping them watered, the wages of

the banana pickers, before they are loaded
carefully on flatbed trucks and driven
to the port where they are carried onto a ship;

the cost of the ship, and the steel workers who
made the steel before the ship was even thought of
and the miners who mined the ore to make the
steel even before that,

and after you have a ship, you have to fuel
that ship to power the huge engines
across the sea to bring the bananas to market
long before they are even ripe,

and what of the men and women who spend
their days involved in some process of making fuel,
and the thousands more who fight and die to preserve
our access to that the fuel that powers the ships
to bring that banana to our shores
only to be unceremoniously eaten without much
thought of the cost in time and treasure of a single,
golden, fifty-nine cent banana that is surely
worth much, much more?

PLANS

Perhaps the problem I have
with knowing what I will be
when I grow up is that I never
made plans to grow up at all—
remembering that adults are
mostly dream killers, and boring,
old ogres with an ax to grind
about anyone who thinks differently,
especially those whose only plan
is to stand on one's head until it looks
as if the coast is clear.

An Atypical Alphabetical Alliteration

I've heard it said that affable anteaters also appreciate apricots while bootybopped bumblebees browse bargains at bookstores and carnivorous catfish create constipated caviar because dingleberried dogies drive dumpy Datsuns as exuberant elephants engage in extramarital examinations, chagrined by fortuitously floppy flanksteaks freaked-out by four-pronged forks and gregarious gringos grappling with gargantuan, grubby gumdrops humorously honoring homosapiens for hysterical humor, indecent incantations, and ignomatic, incontinent imbeciles doing jumping jacks with jerks, jackals and judicious jambalaya chefs kooking kangaroo kebabs while karefully kareening down kanyons, looting lollipops from little lasses looking like lollygaggers making memories at Monster Mashes because neglectful nincompoops negotiate negatively with naughty nightgowns on occasion, opulently occurring on other-worldly orbs while puppies pooping peach pits project problematic quandaries in quick quips, quietly in quasi-queer revolts, running reckless in ravines like ravenous ravens and slinky, slithering sloths superfluously slouching sideways through treacherous and treasonous tumults because underwire underwear in uncomely umber undulates vociferously, and victorious varmints volunteering in wigwams full of wailing wombats waning westward xcitedly xume xenophobic Xeroxes while yonder youths yack the yarns of yellow yoyos on the Zanzibarian zebras of Zebedee who are zealously zipping at the zombie zodiak.

MEMORIES @ 1 AM

It's strange how my mind seems to wander
late at night, when the past forty years seem
to blur together into a goulash of time,
when one minute I can be thinking about the
flavor of those jelly beans I had that one Easter
in Florida when I was ten, and the next minute
I am remembering that today
is my mom's birthday and I ought to call,
but probably after the sun rises, after I try out
those new razors my wife probably paid too much
for and for some reason it leaves me thinking about those
green florescent shoelaces I had in the sixth grade when
such things were hip and are now on the rebound—
thirty years after I fell in love with Sarah Browning,
a really great girl who has three, or is it four children;
I met her husband that time when he came to the studio
to buy a gift for her and we made the connection;
me, remembering the time when my acrobatic stunt
in her kitchen resulted in that dent in the door of her
dishwasher which I was told was still there fifteen years
later when they moved to that ranch in Montana where
her dad got a job counting antelope, under that big sky
that seems so limitless, without horizons to control
the breadth, or jet trails to define it like they do

so often here, especially just after sunset when they burn
in the night sky like a painful scar the never heals,
similar to the one on my belt line from the surgery in
Wisconsin that got infected and caused me to drop fifty
pounds until I looked much sicker than I felt;
all those long days in the summer humidity when I
wondered why I showered at all because I never
really dried out, but those were happy times as hard
as they were, the first time in my life where I was a
minority; a white man among so many shades of brown,
but learning to love them and fit in the best a white boy
can, and that pizzeria just around the corner from our
terrible apartment where ten dollars bought a deep dish
pie, and all the latest REM songs could be played on the
jukebox, including the new song, Everybody Hurts, and
though it is no more true now than it was then, it took
me almost twenty summers to remember the truth about
pain and the burdens we all carry with us like backpacks
full of rocks until someone says, that is enough.

A Jar of Clarity

I opened the jar today;
the one we keep in the window;
the ornate specimen jar;
the one I went looking for
for just this purpose;
the one filled with seashells;
the ones we gathered
on our morning walks
while the kids were still
sleeping and life was filled
with beauty and clarity.

I realized that jar has been
sitting there now for nineteen
months, taunting me each day,
reminding me of those January
mornings when the beach
was ours alone, and the world
was new, and life was filled
with beauty and clarity.

MID-LIFE MEDICINE

I wonder if they have a drug
for mid-life crises—
a sort of pick-me-up
mixed with a butt-kicker

to help one realize how good
they've got it now that the house
is paid off and the drive to work hard
has been diminished,

one's time now occupied with how one
will spend the rest of one's life,
however long it may be,
trying to find purpose and pleasure

in things that don't make much sense
anymore—maybe never really did,
but one went along with it because
it paid the bills, getting one closer
to the goal—that variable, moving target
that made sense one day, but not the next—
a sort of temporary mental illness that you hope
will clear up sometime soon as one struggles
to try to comprehend this passage of time.

All the Magic That Surrounds Us

I never considered that I would have reason
to envy the hobos of the world, but this morning
I find I am still thinking about that man
I saw downtown on the bench last night
with nothing more than his rotund belly,
his walrus mustache, and his backpack
to keep him company as I rushed past him
to the presentation—late as usual.

And how an hour later, when I rushed back
the way I had come, hurrying to make it
to the opening at the gallery
where some of my new work was showing,
I saw him again, still sitting there, alone,
a content smile on his face,
observing the world,

as if he were wondering why
we are all scurrying about at high speed,
thinking, I imagined, how much better life might be
without a watch ruling our days,
hijacking our freedom,
beating us into the dirt if we dare stop
to listen to the rhythmic music of shoes rushing
across the pavement, or to share our crumbs with
the pigeons, or to watch all the silly people hurrying
by so quickly that they forget to stop and recognize
all the magic that surrounds us.

Mapping a Day's Journey

This is the part when I roll out of bed;
putting an unwelcomed end to the dreams of night.

And this is the part where I stand under the water while
reckoning which of the day's tasks need doing most.

This is the part when I put my hands to my work,
just a moment after finishing my morning meal,
having run out of reasons to stall any further.

Then quickly comes the part when the creative ideas
begin flowing, colorful barges and paddleboats on a
crowded stream of consciousness, hurrying to their
destination—some getting stuck on sandbars;
others searching for long-whiskered catfish
among the reeds and dark shadows.

This is the part when I stand at the foothills,
wondering if I have the energy or desire to climb
the mountains of unfinished chores this afternoon.

And this is the part where I pitch my tent
as the sun sets behind me,
which I almost miss—distracted by my thoughts
and regrets of all the things I never got around to doing.

This is the part when I lay down on my bed,
a belly full of trail mix and a backpack full
of the characters of a hundred thousand books,
who meet me at the crossroads to sing me into dreamland,
each hoping theirs will be the song
that keeps me up tonight.

BELOW AVERAGE

I've heard it said that
the average mattress
becomes seven pounds
heavier each year
due to the sloughing off
of dead skin that essentially
embeds itself in the bed.

It's really a disgusting figure
that used to keep me up at night,
but as I moved the mattress today
that we bought when we got
married, seventeen years ago,
I felt quite relieved that my
old mattress was certainly
not a hundred pounds heavier
than when we bought it;
that honeymoon bed
which has seen so many nights
since we first laid down
together, leaving me grateful
that in at least one manner,
we are far below average.

YOGA PANTS

Aren't you glad I still check you out?
I asked through the STEAMED up
shower door after she caught me
watching her slide on her yoga pants
to go for a run.

And she smiled, **acknowledging** that
she did like it that I sill had eyes for her
after nearly seventeen years—
that last *prime* number before
reaching twenty … unless of course
you count nineteen as a prime number too,
which I suppose **most** people do who
remember what prime numbers are—
as INSIGNIFICANT as they may be.

But my reason for writing ***this*** doesn't really
have anything to do with prime numbers at all,
but rather it is JUST TO SAY, I love you,
and I plan on checking you out through
every steamy shower door for the next
fifty prime numbers, regardless of whether
you FIT into those yoga pants OR NOT.

DANDELIONS IN THE SUN

I discovered them
one morning
at the intersection
of Earth and Elysium.

Struck by their singular beauty,
I had to stop
and bare witness
to their magical enchantment—

how, as the golden light gently touched
each tiny filament, they were miraculously
transfigured from ignoble weeds
to magnificent, illuminated apparitions,

leading me to marvel how the intrinsic,
therapeutic power of pure light
converts all that is carnal and dark,
proffering hope and goodness on its wings
of mercy at the dawn of each new day.

AUTUMN'S SEDUCTION

I went out for a ride last night
and came home with the scent
of the wind in my hair;
like lipstick on my collar,
having run wild and free,
flirting with danger—

and discovering once again
those simple, beautiful things you can
experience on a motor scooter
on an autumn evening that you
can't experience in any other way;

like the sweet bouquet of
cottonwood, aspen, willow and pine,
whose leaves and needles mingle
with the cool, shallow water
of the stream, becoming her perfume;

or the way she wantonly rearranges
every follicle of hair on your body
while she introduces you to the all
the winged creatures, large and small, who dance
and play in her lovely, whispered sonnets,

leaving me with no other option
than to be seduced by her ruffled skirts
and carefree demeanor—her chilling embrace
overshadowed by the warmth of her hues and
her gentle, sweet sigh as her wild love escapes
—untamed.

LIVING WITH ITCH

I heard an interview today
with a doctor who compared
chronic itch to chronic pain
and even wrote a book
about his findings

leaving me to wonder if I
have what he is talking about—
that insatiable, chronic itch
somewhere in my soul
that cannot sit still,

and no amount of scratching
can satisfy; the itch to explore,
the itch to create, the itch to discover
and dream, and be.

And I wonder if I might know enough
someday that I might write my own book
for people like me, and those who love them—
all those who are living and sometimes

dying with that itch that only grows
itchier with a scratching,
often intensifying only by movement,
or the passage of time, or the thought of

far away places, or the smell of rain,
or a memory of the sea—
whose only hope of satisfaction
comes from heading off for adventure;

the itch returning immediately and with
a vengeance at the turning about, or the
homeward bound, or thoughts of the piles
of work that awaits, or the smell of stagnant
waters and stale, comfortable places.

EARLY BIRTHDAY

I received two packages
in the mail yesterday;
those poetry books I bought
from that used bookstore
and a couple of bow ties
I found on Ebay.

And though my birthday
is still a month away,
this is just to say I won't
be needing anything this year.
I have taken care of it myself.
I'd let you wrap the packages
up for me, but I couldn't wait.
So thank you for your
thoughtful, early gifts.
They were exactly
what I wanted!

Advice to English Majors

The probability of something going dreadfully wrong
is significantly greater in the execution of a novel than
it would be for a poem—at least a poem of only a few stanzas,
which is why a person who has chosen to write for a hobby,
or in an attempt to make a living, should probably write only
one page novels and very short poems if they ever hope
to avoid both conflict and scrutiny.

Of course, conflict and scrutiny could both be easily avoided
by writing to a particular audience: the heavily demented,
the keenly lethargic, or your doting mother to name a few,
who would likely be a receptive audience, offering little resistance,
but also likely little in terms of constructive feedback.

Which may be a good point when considering why you have chosen
to write at all, or for that matter, why you have chosen to major
in a language you have spoken fluently since birth,
probably thinking it would be an easy A.

This question is particularly poignant when you have tried
your whole life to avoid both conflict and scrutiny,
which leads me to wonder if you might not be better off
in a vocational school, perhaps plumbing, where you will be able
to rescue the distressed and offer hope to the hopeless as you drive
around in your big, white van with catchy little affirmations
emblazoned on the side, things like,

We're number one in a number two business!
helping everyone feel secure and happy,
knowing that if a problem should ever arise,
you will be there, dressed in your cape and mask,
toting your quiver full of oversized wrenches to save the day,
which few, if any, would ever scrutinize as you help
rid the world of conflict and vice.

OVATION

We offered them a standing ovation,
this jolly band of four
who had just performed their
final act of their final concert
on instruments I had never seen
or heard of, their voices harmonized
in such a way that made it seem
they must have played together
much longer than the five short years
before an opportunity on the east coast
and another child would interrupt their
music making indefinitely.

We're sorry, the leader said, but we have
literally just performed every song we
ever wrote, so there won't be an encore.

And I was surprised by the sadness
his announcement conjured,
having so enjoyed the first and last concert
I would ever hear from them,
leaving me wishing they might
have held in reserve, one last ditty
to send us on our way.

Things to Remember

When I don't remember your name,
please, always remember that I love you,
she used to tell the grandkids
before she went to bed
—too soon old.

And the kids remembered that,
and would come to see her
and stand over her tired body
and look into her kind face
and sunken eyes, her skin
still radiant as if illuminated
by bright candle, deep within.

She seldom spoke after she went to bed,
but when she did, her words were kind
and loving, giving all around her a sliver
of hope, that one way or another we would
make it through this trying time and learn
something profound from these years,
watching Dad spend all his time and treasure
—loving her.

And when that bright candle
grew dim and finally burned out,
and her skin changed from
translucent, to ashen, to opaque,
the love she fed us all with her
double-edged wooden spoon
hovered overhead, offering one
last sliver of hope—
that one way or another,
we would make it through this.

Somewhere In Between

I drove past her garden this morning,
filled so full of flowers
that there is never room for weeds
to grow between them.

And I was reminded of last summer,
or perhaps it was the one before that,
when I stopped and talked to her
as she planted new perennials,

when she confided in me, more of a
stranger than a close friend,
that now that her children were off to college,
she was considering a divorce

from her husband
of nearly 30 years;
their love having grown cold
somewhere in between.

And as I drove past her garden
this morning, I found myself wondering
once again what happened to them,
realizing I have not seen him for some time,

leaving me to consider what briars
must have grown between them,
crowding out the love they once shared
while the garden that mattered so much less
remained unencumbered by complications.

So on my way home, I will drop by the florist
and gather up a bouquet of flowers
for my wife in hopes of
warding off any briars

that I occasionally find popping up in the
unattended ground between us when
we have spent too much time in the garden of
inconsequential and significantly lesser things.

About the Artist

Over the past two and half decades, I have learned that the path an artist walks is rarely straight and infrequently narrow, but generally vibrant, outrageously colorful, and full of surprises. I have learned again and again that we are our only legitimate limitations, and that our dreams should be big enough to keep us inspired and striving. I recognize that my life has been a series of accidents that have somehow been mercifully and miraculously customized and timed to occur at the exact moment they need to. In the process, I have learned that life itself is poetry—art in glorious motion—waiting for us to recognize its beauty and magnificence.

Though I still make my living primarily as a potter, I have found that there is much more to our lives than how we pay our bills. For me, this includes an insatiable itch to create, to play, and to discover. That itch has served me well, filling my life with curiosity and giving light to my path as I work on figuring out who I am.

I was fortunate enough to marry to the one woman on earth who would not only allow me to pursue my dreams, but also encourage me in it. Lynnette and I were married in 1997, and we are the proud parents of two crazy kids, Isaac and Eve. We live at the foothills of the Wasatch Mountains where we love to hike, ski, and fly fish.

In the Summer of 2014, we spent six weeks in Italy, Germany, Switzerland and France. Most of the photography and many of the poems included in this book were inspired by that grand adventure.

It took me nearly twelve years to write my first book, Remembering Isaac. With this one, I now have seven books, including Discovering Isaac, Becoming Isaac, Forget-me- Notes, Borrowing Fire, and Put a Cherry on Top, all of which are available from Amazon and wherever above average books are sold.

At least seven other literary projects are currently in the process of being hatched. Stay tuned to my progress at www.benbehunin.blogspot.com

Thanks for reading. Cheers

Personalized books can be ordered at
www.potterboy.com

Please register on the email mailing list to
receive notices and updates about future
publications and pottery shows.

Ben enjoys hearing from his readers.
Please send correspondence to

Abendmahl Press
P.O. Box 581083
Salt Lake City, Utah 84158-1083
or by email to benbehunin@comcast.net

More information on this book and others is
available at www.benbehunin.blogspot.com

Ben's pottery is available at www.potterboy.com
and in many fine galleries across the USA

If you would like to feature any of Ben's books at your book club,
please contact him for a group discount.

For speaking engagements, please call (801) 883-0146

For design inquiries, contact Bert Compton
at bert@comptonds.com